A FIELD GUIDE TO
Washington, D.C.

PHOTOGRAPHY BY JAKE MCGUIRE AND ANNA KATALKINA
NARRATIVE BY NICHOLE WADSWORTH SCHRAFFT

First published in the United States
of America by:

Twin Lights Publishers, Inc.
8 Hale Street
Rockport, Massachusetts 01966
Telephone: (978) 546-7398
http://www.twinlightspub.com

ISBN 13: 978-1-885435-97-2
ISBN 10: 1-885435-97-5

10 9 8 7 6 5 4 3 2 1

Images listed below are courtesy of the
Smithsonian's National Museum of
American History

Page 4 - Lincoln's top hat
Page 16 - Dorothy's ruby slippers
Page 19 - FDR's microphone
Page 29 - Kermit the Frog
Page 31 - Lewis & Clark's compass

Images listed below are courtesy of the
Smithsonian's National Air and Space Museum

Page 6 - Apollo Lunar Module II
Page 35 - Milestone of Flight Gallery
Page 64 - 1903 Wright Flyer
Page 65 - North American X-15
Page 65 - Bell X-1 piloted by Chuck Yeager

Book design by
SYP Design & Production, Inc.
http://www.sypdesign.com

Printed in China

As both a teacher and a mother to an increasingly curious one and a half year old, I am inspired, or possibly doomed, to always look for the lesson to be learned from any activity...no matter how small. A trip to the grocery store can become a lesson in marketing, nutrition, or economics; a trip to the park becomes an explosion of botany, horticulture, and entomology; and a quick stop at the pharmacy begs to be turned into an excuse to introduce all of the systems of the human body. So, just imagine how much can be learned in a city as historically and culturally rich as Washington, D.C.

Ideally this book will serve as your guide as you explore each nuance of this amazing city, but fear not, because even if you can not actually get to Washington, D.C. there is so much to be learned by reading through its pages. Surely the strikingly beautiful photos will make you feel as if you were truly there. From a carousel to the Commander-in-Chief, dinosaurs to Democrats, Kermit the Frog to the Kennedy Center, *Marine One* to Mastodons, and Secret Service to the *Spirit of St. Louis*, this book takes you on an amazing educational adventure. I can't think of a better way to give your child an overview of the American political system and a great respect for all who have served to protect our country while also sparking their interest in the arts, history, and the sciences. I hope you learn as much by reading this book as I did by writing it!

—Nichole Wadswroth Schrafft

ABRAHAM LINCOLN MEMORIAL

A memorial to the nation's 16th President. The Lincoln Memorial was designed after Greek architecture and has 38 columns that represent the 38 states that were a part of the Union at the time of Lincoln's death. Inside the monument sits a 19-foot-high and 175-ton statue of the President. The words to Lincoln's second inaugural speech and the Gettysburg Address are also carved inside the moment.

ABRAHAM LINCOLN'S TOP HAT

This top hat was worn by President Lincoln the night he was assassinated by John Wilkes Booth at the Ford's Theater in 1865. Booth was captured two weeks later and shot by Union soldiers. The top hat is in the collection of the Smithsonian's National Museum of American History.

AFRICAN BUSH ELEPHANT

A focal point in the rotunda of the Smithsonian's National Museum of Natural History. This African Bush Elephant is the largest on record with a weight of 27,000 pounds and almost 14 feet high when it was shot in Angola. It is now mounted in the museum for all to see.

AIR FORCE MEMORIAL

A memorial that honors the members of the United States Air Force and the organizations that came before it. Three stainless steel spires reach up into the sky as high as 270 feet. The spires represent flying and the three core values of the Air Force; "intergrity first, service before self, and excellence in all that is done." They also honor the three strands of the Air Force: the active, the guard, and the reserve.

AIR FORCE ONE

The name given to the United States Air Force aircraft that transports the President. There are two specially designed and customized Boeing aircrafts in the Presidential Fleet and when the President is on board the air traffic control name for the plane is "Air Force One."

AMBASSADOR

A high-ranking diplomat who represents one country while residing in another. Washington, D.C. is home to ambassadors from all over the world who serve to represent their homeland in the United States.

AMENDMENT

A change to a document, bill, motion, or the United States Constitution.

AMERICAN FLAG

A symbol of the United States of America's strength and unity. Today's flag has 13 alternating red and white stripes that represent the original 13 colonies and 50 white stars that represent the 50 states. The first official flag was approved by the Continental Congress on June 14, 1777.

AMERICAN RED CROSS

Employees and volunteers have been serving overseas since 1892. "The Red Cross Spirit" is a memorial to all who have given their lives while serving with the American Red Cross.

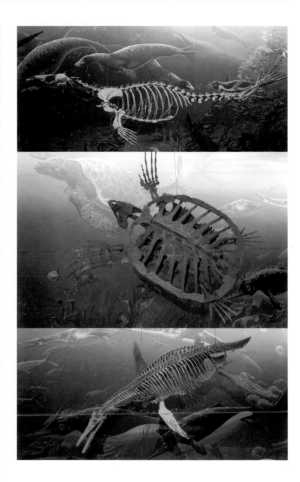

ANCIENT SEAS

An exhibit at the Smithsonian's National Museum of Natural History that tells the history of 540 million years of marine life. The Ancient Seas exhibit describes the extinctions and evolutions from the Paleozoic Era (540 to 250 million years ago) to the Cenozoic Era (65 million years ago to today).

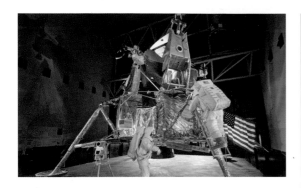

APOLLO LUNAR MODULE 11

This lunar module at the Smithsonian's Air and Space Museum is similar to the *Eagle* used in 1969 when Neil Armstrong became the first man to walk on the moon. As he put his left foot down, Armstrong uttered the now famous words, "That's one small step for man, one giant leap for mankind." At the landing site, Armstrong and fellow astronaut, "Buzz" Aldrin left behind an American flag, a patch honoring the fallen *Apollo 1* crew, and a plaque on one of *Eagle*'s legs. It reads, "Here men from the planet Earth first set foot upon the moon. July 1969 A.D. We came in peace for all mankind."

ARLINGTON MEMORIAL BRIDGE

A bridge that crosses the Potomac River connecting the Arlington House and the Lincoln Memorial. The bridge is 2,163 feet long and is often called Washington's most beautiful bridge.

ARLINGTON NATIONAL CEMETERY

An American military cemetery where over 300,000 have been laid to rest. Veterans from every American war have been buried within the cemetery's amazing 624 acres. Two American Presidents, William Taft and John F. Kennedy, have been buried here along with many other notable people such as astronauts, explorers, chief justices, 3,800 liberated slaves, and the unknown soldiers. Funerals are conducted Monday–Friday with over 20 people buried each day and about 5,400 each year.

ARTICLES OF CONFEDERATION

The first Constitution of the United States. The Articles of Confederation were written in 1777 and went into effect in 1781 after being ratified, or signed, by the 13 colonies. The first President of Congress after the Articles of Confederation were adopted was Samuel Huntington. The U.S. Constitution replaced the Articles of Confederation when it was adopted on September 17, 1787.

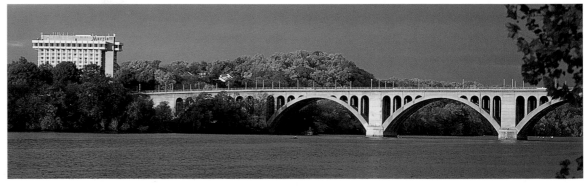

BASILICA OF THE NATIONAL SHRINE

The largest church in the western hemisphere and the 7th largest religious structure in the entire world. The Basilica is a catholic church that is also a National Historic Landmark.

BEAD MUSEUM

The Bead Museum, with over 5,000 items, strives to interpret the significance and usage of beads in cultures over time. Beads are among mankind's earliest creative achievements and have been used as amulets of protection, symbols of status, and personal ornaments.

BENJAMIN FRANKLIN STATUE

One of the most important founding fathers of the United States and one of the five men chosen to draft the Declaration of Independence, Benjamin Franklin was a writer, a politician, a scientist, and an inventor. He had many great accomplishments during his life. He started the first volunteer fire department and the American Philosophical Society. He also wrote and published *Poor Richard's Almanac.* As an inventor he is responsible for the invention of bifocals, the odometer, the Franklin Stove, and the lightning rod. This statue of Benjamin Franklin stands in the Federal Triangle.

BILL

A piece of legislation that goes to the House of Representatives and the Senate with hopes of being made into a law. Anyone can write a bill, but only a member of Congress can introduce it. A bill must go through quite a process before being accepted, if it ever is. Many bills "die in committee" when they are rejected and not acted upon.

BILL OF RIGHTS

In 1789 twelve amendments to the Constitution were proposed, but the first two were not ratified, leaving just ten. Those ten amendments sought to protect the rights of United States citizens and became known as the Bill of Rights. One of the original copies can be seen in the National Archives.

BISMARK SAPPHIRE

One of the world's largest sapphires. The Bismark Sapphire is a 98.6 carat gem that was found in Sri Lanka. The gem was given to the Smithsonian's National Museum of Natural History by Countess Mona von Bismark in 1967.

BUDGET

A financial plan for the federal government proposed by the President each February. The budget needs to include money to be spent in areas such as defense, energy, health, agriculture, transportation, international affairs, and space and technology.

BULLION

A mass of precious metals. American Eagle platinum, gold, and silver bullion coins can be purchased through the United States Mint.

BUREAU OF ENGRAVING AND PRINTING

The government agency that prints paper money. An average of about 3 ½ billion one dollar bills are printed each year. The Bureau of Engraving and Printing also prints stamps and important government papers.

BUTTERFLY HABITAT GARDEN

An exhibit at the Smithsonian's National Museum of Natural History that shows the relationship between plants and butterflies. The Butterfly Habitat Garden was created in 1995 and became the museum's first outdoor habitat. The garden actually includes four different habitats and has been visited by close to 30 species of butterflies.

C & O Canal Boat Ride

The National Parks Service operates boat rides, pulled by mules, along the Chesapeake and Ohio Canal. Tourists experience rising in an eight foot lock and learn about how life was like on the canal from park rangers dressed in period clothing.

Cabinet

A part of the executive branch of the federal government that includes heads of 15 federal executive departments. The heads of those departments are chosen by the President with approval from the U.S. Senate.

Capitalism

An economic system that allows people, companies, or corporations to own means of production rather than having the government own everything.

CAPITOL

The capitol building serves as the seat of government for the legislative branch of the United States Congress. The building has a central dome located above a rotunda and two wings. The north wing is the Senate chamber and the south wing is the House of Representatives chamber.

CAPITOL HILL

The largest historic residential neighborhood in Washington, D.C. and also a name used to refer to the Congress.

CAROUSEL ON THE MALL

A 1947 vintage carousel that can be enjoyed on the National Mall.

CHANGING OF THE GUARD

The Tomb of the Unknown Soldier at Arlington National Cemetery is guarded 24 hours a day, 365 days a year. An unidentified soldier from World War I, World War II, the Korean War, and the Vietnam War are actually buried in the tomb. The Unknown Soldier from the Vietnam War was later identified as Michael J. Blassie. Members of the 3rd U.S. Infantry must meet strict criteria and pass a series of difficult tests in order to have the honor of being a sentinel at the tomb. While being led by a relief commander, one sentinel replaces another in an elaborate and very precise ceremony called the Changing of the Guard.

CHECKS AND BALANCES

A system designed so the three branches of government maintain an equal amount of power, thus allowing no one branch to become too powerful. The Legislative, Judicial, and Executive branches of government each have different responsibilities that give them control over the other branches.

CHERRY BLOSSOM

In 1912 Washington, D.C. received a gift of 3,000 cherry blossom trees from Mayor Yukio Ozaki of Tokyo. The gift was meant to help celebrate the growing friendship between the U.S. and Japan. To give thanks, the United States gave flowering dogwood trees to Japan. The annual National Cherry Blossom Festival commemorates the gift giving.

CHINATOWN

One entrance to Chinatown is this 75-foot-wide "Friendship Arch." Its center panel is inscribed with Chinese characters which read *zhongguo cheng*, meaning Chinese city. Today, the Wok & Roll restaurant occupies what was once Mary Surratt's boarding house - the meeting place for John Wilkes Booth and his conspirators in Abraham Lincoln's assassination.

CHRISTOPHER COLUMBUS STATUE

Columbus and his famous journey of discovery are honored in a variety of ways throughout the nation's capital. A fountain at Union Station is dedicated to his honor and is inscribed with the words, "To the memory of Christopher Columbus whose high faith and indomitable courage gave to mankind a new world." In front of the statue and fountain stand three flagpoles that represent the three ships that sailed with Columbus on his voyage to the New World. An eagle sits proudly on top of each flagpole.

CIVIL LIBERTIES

Freedoms that protect citizens from being controlled by the government. In the United States the Constitution states what freedoms need to be upheld by our government.

CIVIL WAR

A war fought from 1861-1865 between the northern states belonging to the Union and the southern states that had formed the Confederacy. In the end the North was victorious and slavery was ended while the Union remained intact. An African American Civil War Memorial called "The Spirit of Freedom" can be seen on the corner of 10th and U Street.

COMMANDER-IN-CHIEF

The President of the United States is also the commander of all of the country's military forces giving him the title of Commander-in-Chief.

CONGRESS

The legislative branch of the United States federal government primarily responsible for making laws. Congress is made up of the House of Representatives, also called the Lower House, and the Senate, also called the Upper House. Amongst other things, Congress votes on bills, passes laws after debating and taking a vote, decides how to spend the country's budget, and shapes foreign policy.

CONGRESSIONAL GOLD MEDAL

The highest award and honor that can be presented to a person who performs an outstanding act of service beneficial to the country. The legislative branch of the US federal government is responsible for bestowing this award.

CONSERVATIVE

A citizen who typically does not like change in the laws and regulations that effect their lives or how the country is run. Conservatives are often called "right-winged."

CONSTITUTION

The supreme law of the United States. The Constitution was completed on September 17, 1787. A copy of the Constitution is on display at the National Archives.

DAUGHTERS OF THE AMERICAN REVOLUTION MUSEUM

A museum founded by women in 1890 who were annoyed from being excluded from men's patriotic organizations. The museum preserves the heritage of American Independence with a collection of over 30,000 historic relics.

DECLARATION OF INDEPENDENCE

The document that declared the original 13 colonies to be free from Great Britain. It was adopted on July 4, 1776 and is the reason we celebrate the 4th of July as Independence Day. The Declaration of Independence can be seen at the National Archives and Records Administration in the Rotunda for the Charters of Freedom.

DEMOCRATIC PARTY

One of the two major political parties in the United States. The symbol for the Democratic Party is a donkey. Andrew Jackson was the 7th President of the United States, but was the first Democratic President.

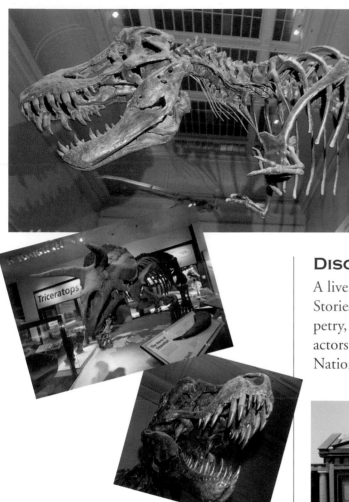

DISTRICT OF COLUMBIA

The federal district within the nation's capital city. The city is named after President George Washington while the "Columbia" in "District of Columbia" pays tribute to Christopher Columbus.

DISCOVERY THEATER

A live theatre aimed to entertain children. Stories and folktales are told through puppetry, storytellers, dancers, musicians, and actors. The fun can be seen on the National Mall at Ripley Center.

DONALD W. REYNOLDS CENTER FOR AMERICAN ART AND PORTRAITURE

The National Portrait Gallery and Smithsonian American Art Museum are collectively known as the Donald W. Reynolds Center for American Art and Portraiture. The Portrait Gallery includes photographs and videos of all the presidents, while the American Art Museum displays more than 3,000 of its 41,000 pieces.

DINOSAUR HALL

A permanent exhibit at the Smithsonian's National Museum of Natural History. The exhibit includes life-size dinosaurs such as the *allosaurus* and *diplodocus*, Life in the Ancient Sea, Fossil Mammals, and Fossil Plants.

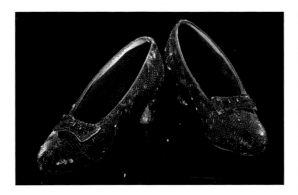

DOROTHY'S RUBY SLIPPERS

The magic slippers that helped Dorothy get back home to Kansas in *The Wizard of OZ*. These petite size 5 slippers were worn by Judy Garland during the filming of this 1939 classic. The ruby slippers are in the collection of the Smithsonian's National Museum of American History.

DR. MARTIN LUTHER KING, JR. LIBRARY

Named after Dr. Martin Luther King Jr., the central building for the DC Public Library opened in 1972. Built with black steel and dark tinted glass, the library's modern architecture is unique to the rest of the city. A large mural of MLK is painted across the walls of the library.

DULLES AIRPORT

Officially called Washington-Dulles International Airport, Dulles is located about 25 miles outside of the city of Washington and handles about 2,000 flights each day.

DUPONT CIRCLE

A traffic circle located at the intersection of five Washington, D.C. streets. A small public park with a fountain is located in the center of Dupont Circle and the neighborhood surrounding the circle is the home to many embassies.

ECONOMY

The country's system of producing, distributing, and consuming goods. Typically when people refer to the economy they are speaking about the country's financial situation.

EINSTEIN STATUE

A bronze statue of Albert Einstein sitting with papers in his hand on the property of the National Academy of Sciences. The statue weighs 7,000 pounds.

ELECTION

A process during which a vote is taken and the person with the highest number wins. Presidential elections are held every four years and begin with primaries, caucuses, and national conventions which whittle the field of candidates down to one from each party. The remaining candidates then select a running mate who would become Vice President if they were to win. Campaigning occurs until November of the election year, at which time the American public votes. Those votes are counted and become known as the "popular vote."

Electoral College

Each state receives a number of "electoral votes" which are based on its number of US Representatives plus its 2 US Senators. Each state has a different number of Electoral Votes. After the Presidential elections, the electors of each state cast their votes for President. Electors will often cast their vote for the candidate that received the most votes in their state. However, it is not illegal for them to vote contrary to that decision. The winner from this vote is sworn into the President's office in January.

Ellipse

A 52-acre park that is officially named The President's Park South. It is commonly called "The Ellipse" because of its shape. Located at the far end of the White House's lawn, it was originally used as a campsite for Union soldiers and a place to keep cattle and horses during the Civil War.

Embassy Row

Washington's Massachusetts Avenue is home to many foreign embassies and has been given the nickname "Embassy Row."

Executive Branch

One of the three branches of the Federal Government. The Executive Branch enforces and executes laws. It consists of the President, the President's staff, executive agencies, and cabinet members.

FBI Building

Officially named the J. Edgar Hoover Federal Bureau of Investigation, this building is the headquarters for the FBI. When tours are open, visitors can see FBI agents at work in the forensics laboratory, giving firearm demonstrations and exhibits on fingerprinting, DNA analysis, confiscated weapons, and more.

Federal Government

All aspects and departments of the United States government. Towns, cities, and states have their own independent governments, but the federal government oversees the activity of the country as a whole.

FEDERAL JUDGES

Judges appointed by the President and follow the guidelines written in Article III of the Constitution. Federal judges serve for life as long as they are practicing good behavior.

FEDERAL RESERVE SYSTEM

The central bank of the United States. The main responsibility of the bank is to maintain the national currency and money supply. It also sets the official interest rate to control inflation and the exchange rate.

FEDERALISTS

The group of people who supported the ratification of the Constitution beginning in 1787. Today's federalists are in favor of independent states having control over issues and making their own policies that may be different from what other states decide to do rather than having the federal government make the exact same laws for all 50 states.

FIRESIDE CHAT MICROPHONE

Franklin D. Roosevelt delivered more than 30 broadcasts, known at "fireside chats," between 1933 and 1944. These chats enabled him to build confidence in his leadership and a rapport with the American people during the Great Depression and World War II. The microphone is in the collection of the Smithsonian's National Museum of American History.

FIRST DIVISION MONUMENT

This monument, located in Presidents Park, pays tribute to the U.S. Army's First Division, who lost their lives during World War I. The statue that tops the 65-foot column is called *Winged Victory*.

FOGGY BOTTOM

One of Washington, D.C.'s oldest neighborhoods. Foggy Bottom got its name because it is located along the marshy banks of the Potomac River where mist and fog tended to gather when that area was still a port. Today, Foggy Bottom is home to many of Washington's important sites and is full of activity.

FOLGER SHAKESPEARE LIBRARY

A research center that is home to the largest collection of Shakespeare materials and other books, manuscripts, and art from the Renaissance period. The Library is on Capitol Hill.

FORD'S THEATRE

A working theatre that is also a tribute to President Lincoln's love of theatre. Ford's Theatre is where Abraham Lincoln was assassinated in 1865. The theatre shut down for 103 years after that tragic event, but reopened in 1968 and has been a favorite spot to visit ever since.

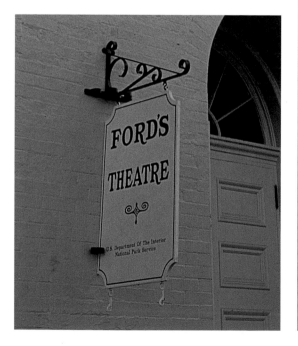

FRANCIS SCOTT KEY BRIDGE

A concrete arch bridge that carries traffic over the Potomac River. Construction of the bridge started in 1917 and was finished in 1923. The bridge was named after Francis Scott Key, author of *The Star Spangled Banner*.

FRANKLIN D. ROOSEVELT MEMORIAL

A memorial located near the Tidal Basin that pays tribute to the country's 32nd President. Four outdoor rooms represent each of his terms of office and the events that occurred during that time.

FREEDOM PLAZA

An open plaza designed in 1980 and named in honor of Martin Luther King, Jr. who happened to work on his famous "I Have a Dream" speech at a hotel nearby. The street plan for the city of Washington is represented in the stones that create the plaza. In 1988 a time capsule that contains a bible, MLK Jr.'s robe, and some of his other belongings was buried in the plaza.

FREEDOM STATUE

The *Statue of Freedom* was created by Thomas Crawford. This bronze statue has adorned the top of the U.S. Capitol dome since 1863. The original name of the sculpture was *Freedom Triumphant in War and Peace.*

FRIENDSHIP 7

Astronaut John Glen piloted the *Friendship 7* during the Mercury 6 Mission. This mission was the first time the United States had attempted to put a human into orbit. On February 20th, 1962 Glenn became the first person to orbit the earth. The *Friendship 7* is on display at the Smithsonian's National Air and Space Museum.

GARGOYLES

These gargoyles adorn the exterior of the National Cathedral. Over 100 mischievous gargoyles direct rainwater away from the National Cathedral. Each gargoyle has its own unique story behind it.

GENERAL ROBERT E. LEE MEMORIAL

During the Civil War General Lee became the most celebrated officer of the Confederate Army. The home that he and his family lived in for 30 years was taken by the Union Army, but after the war the Supreme Court voted to return the home because it was taken without due process. That home, the Arlington House, now stands as the General Robert E. Lee Memorial.

GEORGE MASON MEMORIAL

This bronze statue is a tribute to George Mason, the author of the Virginia Declaration of Rights. Mason was the first to speak up for American liberties and it is said that Thomas Jefferson was motivated by Mason's words when composing the Declaration of Independence. He is remembered for refusing to sign the United States Constitution because it did not abolish slavery and did not grant citizens enough personal liberties.

GEORGE WASHINGTON MEMORIAL

One of two equestrian statues of George Washington located in the Foggy Bottom section of the city. Clark Mills completed the memorial statue of Lieutenant General Washington in 1860, almost 72 years after it was commissioned. This bronze statue, mounted on a sandstone base, stands in the center of a rotary off Pennsylvania Ave.

GEORGETOWN

A neighborhood along the waterfront of the Potomac River. Many politicians have chosen to live in the Georgetown area.

GEORGETOWN UNIVERSITY

The oldest Roman Catholic and Jesuit university in the United States. The university has just about 7,000 undergraduate students and 7,000 graduate students. It takes up over 100 acres of the Georgetown neighborhood of Washington.

GETTYSBURG ADDRESS

A speech given by President Abraham Lincoln at the dedication of the Soldiers' National Cemetery in Gettysburg, Pennsylvania. Although the speech is only 269 words and was delivered in just two short minutes, it has become known as one of the greatest speeches given in American history. Lincoln's speech began, "Four score and seven years ago our fathers brought forth to this continent a new nation, conceived in Liberty, and dedicated to the proposition that all men are created equal."

HOMELAND SECURITY

The term used for the efforts to keep the United States safe from terrorist threats or attacks and also its efforts to respond to national disasters. The Office of Homeland Security was established withing the Executive Office of the President on October 8, 2001.

HOPE DIAMOND

A 45.52 carat blue diamond estimated to be worth between 200 million and 250 million dollars. Legend says that the Hope Diamond puts a curse on the person in possession of it. The Hope Diamond can be traced through the Hope family in London for about 80 years before landing in the United States. It is now part of the National Gem Collection at the Smithsonian's National Museum of Natural History.

HOUSE OF REPRESENTATIVES

One of the two chambers of the United States Congress. Each state has representatives in the House and there are a total of 435 in all. States are given a certain number of representatives depending on their population. States with more citizens get more representatives than states with a smaller population. The House of Representatives meets in the United States Capitol and the Speaker of the House is its presiding officer. Amongst other responsibilities, the House has the ability to impeach officials, elect the President in the case of an Electoral College tie, and initiate revenue bills.

I APPROVE THIS MESSAGE

Under the Bipartisan Campaign Reform Act (BCRA) of 2002, a required phrase said by candidates in political advertisements who are running for federal office. This provision requires a candidate to take responsibility for their campaign adds thereby discouraging them from making controversial claims.

IMAX THEATER

Short for Image Maximum, IMAX theaters use giant screens that are usually a few stories high to create crystal clear, quality images. Surround sound, huge rolls of film, and special projectors and cameras are also used to help create this intense movie viewing experience. IMAX theaters can be found at the Smithsonian's National Museum of Natural History and the National Air and Space Museum, and the Steven F. Udvar-Hazy Center.

INCUMBENT

A candidate who currently holds an elected position and is running for reelection.

INDEPENDENCE DAY

A federal holiday that celebrates the adoption of The Declaration of Independence and the independence of the original 13 colonies from Great Britian's government. Independence Day falls on the 4th of July. More people attend the Independence Day celebrations in Washington, D.C. than any other in the country. There is a parade on Constitution Avenue, cultural celebrations at the Smithsonian Folklife Festival on the National Mall, and then spectacular fireworks over the Washington Monument.

INTERNATIONAL SPY MUSEUM

An exciting museum where visitors get to explore the world of espionage, check out over 200 gadgets used by spies, assume a hidden identity, see the credentials that agents need to get in and out of the country, test their skills of observation and surveillance at interactive stations, see how today's satellites help track spies, learn about how spies have been apprehended or, in some cases, how they are still alluding authorities, and much, much more.

IRS BUILDING

Home to the Internal Revenue Service. The IRS is the United States Federal Government Agency that collects taxes and enforces laws applying to internal revenue. The IRS building is on Constitution Avenue in Washington.

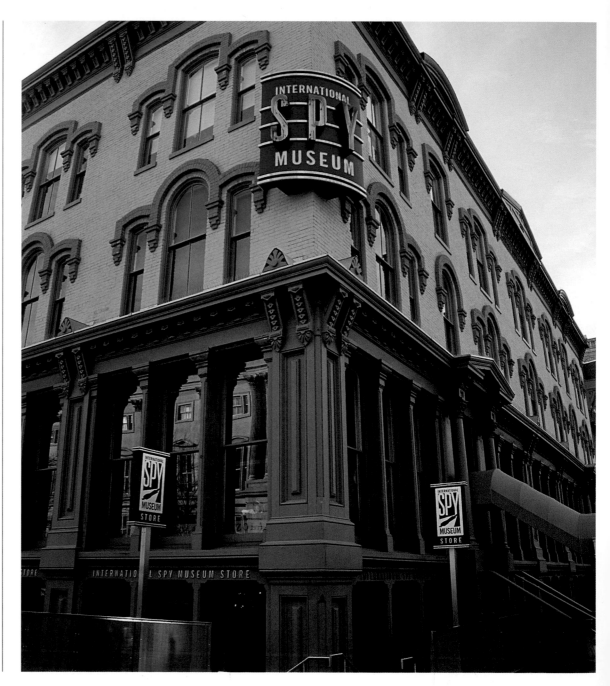

IWO JIMA MEMORIAL

This United States Marine Corps War Memorial pays tribute to the World War II Battle of Iwo Jima and all members of the Marines who have lost their lives during service. The statue is based on a famous photograph that shows six marines raising the American flag after capturing the island. Of the six soldiers in the memorial, only three survived the war.

JAMES A. GARFIELD MONUMENT

This monument honors the 20th President of the United States who was elected in 1880 and assassinated four months later. At the base of the cylindrical pedestal are four large bronze figures, each representing a phase of his career.

JOHN ERICSSON STATUE

John Ericsson is best known for his design of the iron-clad ship, the *Monitor*, which defeated the Confederate ship the *Merrimac* during the Civil War. This crucial invention considerably aided in the defeat of the Southern states.

JOHN F. KENNEDY GRAVESITE

President John Fitzgerald Kennedy was assassinated in Dallas, Texas while riding in an open motorcade with his wife at his side. He was fatally shot on November 22, 1963. JFK was buried in the Arlington National Cemetery three days later.

JUDICIAL BRANCH

One of the three branches of the Federal Government. It is made up of the court system. The highest court in the Judicial Branch is the Supreme Court. The court deals with matters that involve the government, disputes between states, and explaining the Constitution. The Judicial Branch can nullify laws that they decide are unconstitutional and create precedent for future laws and decisions. Decisions made by the Supreme Court are final.

JUSTITIA OMNIBUS

This has been the motto of Washington, D.C. since 1871. *Justitia Omnibus* means "justice for all."

★★★ **K** ★★★

KENNEDY CENTER FOR THE PERFORMING ARTS

A living memorial to John F. Kennedy and the National Center for Performing Arts. It is the nation's busiest art facility and has more than 3,000 performances annually. Each year the Kennedy Center honors five people who have made a significant contribution to the arts.

KENNEDY, ROBERT

The 64th Attorney General of the United States and younger brother of John F. Kennedy. Also called RFK, Robert Kennedy was assassinated on June 5th, 1968 at the beginning of his own run for Presidency. Robert Kennedy was buried near his brother in Arlington National Cemetery.

KERMIT THE FROG

This beloved frog made his television debut on the Washington, D.C. show, *Sam and Friends*. Performed by creator Jim Henson until his death in 1990, Kermit first appeared on *Sesame Street* in 1969 and the *Muppet Show* in 1976. He is in the collection of the Smithsonian's National Museum of American History.

KIDS FARM

An educational interactive exhibit at the National Zoo. Children learn how most of the food they eat comes from farms and how much effort it takes to look after the animals that provide them with food. They can learn about cows, ducks, chickens, donkeys, goats, and also how pizza ingredients are grown.

KING, MARTIN LUTHER

A leader of the Civil Rights Movement. Martin Luther King, Jr. dedicated his lifetime to fighting for equal rights for all races and became the youngest person ever to be honored with a Noble Peace Prize for his dedication to nonviolence. MKL's famous "I Have a Dream" speech was delivered on the steps of the Lincoln Memorial in 1963. In 1968, Martin Luther King, Jr. was assassinated in Memphis, Tennessee. The site for the memorial is between the Lincoln and Jefferson Memorials on the National Mall.

KOREAN WAR MEMORIAL

A memorial to all of the soldiers who participated in the Korean War. Nineteen statues of soldiers on patrol represent members of the US Air Force, Army, Navy, and Marines coming together for a common goal. A 164-foot granite wall is sandblasted with over 2,000 photographs of support troops who aided in the effort along with the words, "Freedom is Not Free." Visitors can sit quietly by the Pool of Remembrance and pay respect to the 54,246 lives that were lost.

★★★ L ★★★

LAFAYETTE PARK

A seven acre public park located directly in front of the White House. The park was originally named President's Park, but was renamed in 1824 to honor General Layfayette of France. The park has been used as many things such as a graveyard, a racetrack, a zoo, a slave market, an encampment for soldiers during the War of 1812, and a venue for political protests.

LEGISLATIVE BRANCH

One of the three branches of the United States Federal Government. The Legislative Branch includes Congress, which is made up of the House of Representatives and the Senate. The Legislative Branch is responsible for making acts into laws and they also have the power to impeach the President, override presidential veto, confirm presidential appointments, and control the budget.

L'ENFANT, PIERRE

The architect who proposed the first street plan for the city of Washington, D.C. L'Enfant submitted his plan to George Washington in 1791. A copy of L'Enfant's original plans is kept at the Library of Congress.

LEWIS AND CLARKS' COMPASS

Meriwether Lewis and William Clark led the Corps of Discovery on an expedition to the American Northwest in 1804. Visitors can see a silver-plated pocket compass that was used during the expedition on display at the Smithsonian's National Museum of American History.

LIBERTY

Personal freedom. The last line of The Pledge of Allegiance is "with liberty and justice for all."

LIBRARY OF CONGRESS

The largest library in the world and the research facility for Congress. The library occupies three buildings on Capitol Hill.

31

MADISON, DOLLEY

The wife of President James Madison. The house where Dolley spent the last 12 years of her life still stands at the corner of Madison Place and H Street.

MAGNA CARTA

Magna Carta, meaning Great Charter, is a 1215 charter guarantying rights and liberties to all freemen by the king of England to his subjects. It is one of the most important legal documents in the history of democracy and greatly influenced the United States Constitution and The Bill of Rights.

MAHATMA GANDHI MEMORIAL

The Mahatma Gandhi Memorial is located across the street from the Indian Embassy. Gandhi was a major political and spiritual leader of India who was committed to peaceful resistance in the fight against injustice. Ghandi was assassinated in New Deli at the age of 78.

MARINE ONE

Marine Helicopter Squadron One, nick-named "Marine One" is the helicopter responsible for transporting the President of the United States and other VIPs. The United States Marine Corps has been responsible for presidential transportation since 1976.

MASTODON

The American Mastodon was a massive herbivore whose habitat stretched from the Atlantic to the Pacific coasts of North America, and from Alaska down to Central America. Visitors to the Smith-sonian's National Museum of Natural History can view a skeleton of the masto-don at the Ice Age Mammals exhibit.

METRO

Washington's subway system. The Metro first opened in 1976 with about 4 ½ miles of track and today covers over 106 miles with 86 subway stops.

MONARCHY

A form of government in which the leader is not voted into office, but instead inherits the position for life.

MONEY

The official currency of a nation. The currency used in the United States is called the dollar. Paper money or bills are produced at the Bureau of Engraving and Printing while coins are produced at the National Mint. The first US dollar was issued in 1862.

MOUNT VERNON

Home to George Washington from 1747 until his death in 1799. The 40-acre estate overlooks the Potomac River in Alexandria, Virginia, just south of Washington, D.C. George and Martha Washington are buried on the property. The house has been restored and has much of the original furniture and family belongings. It is open daily for tours.

NATIONAL AIR AND SPACE MUSEUM

Home to the largest historic air and space-craft collection in the world with more than 50,000 artifacts. Visited by more than nine million people each year, it is said that the Air and Space Museum is the most popular museum in Washington, D.C. and the world. The Air and Space Museum is a part of the Smithsonian Institute.

NATIONAL AQUARIUM

The oldest aquarium in the United States. The aquarium has 50 tanks that are home to over 1,000 creatures including sea turtles, sharks, and Crunch and Munch, the resident alligators.

NATIONAL GALLERY OF ART

One of the finest collections of art in the world. The National Gallery of Art was created by Congress with a large donation of art from Andrew W. Mellon. The National Gallery of Art has two buildings, the East and West buildings, as well as a large sculpture garden with over six acres of art.

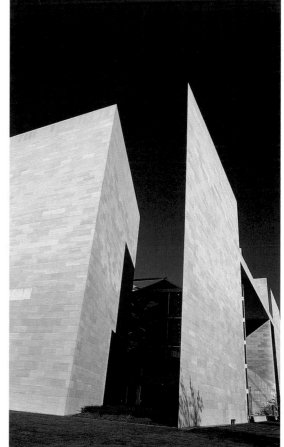

NATIONAL ARBORETUM

Four hundred and forty-six acres of gardens filled with plants, trees, flowers, and herbs administered by the U.S. Department of Agriculture's Agricultural Research Service. Some of the major gardens include the Asian Collection, Fern Valley, and the Azalea and Dogwood Collections.

NATIONAL ARCHIVES

The agency responsible for preserving and documenting government and historical records. The National Archives also makes some of those documents available for the public to see. Some of the documents available for viewing are the US Constitution, the Bill of Rights, the Declaration of Independence, the Louisiana Purchase, and the Emancipation Proclamation.

NATIONAL GEOGRAPHIC EXPLORERS HALL MUSEUM

A museum where National Geographic expeditions and adventures come to life for visitors. Artifacts, photographs, art, and scientific research make visitors feel like they've joined National Geographic on a real life expedition.

NATIONAL MALL

A two-mile strip of grass surrounded by some of Washington's most important landmarks such as the Capitol Building, Washington Monument, Ulysses S. Grant Monument, and many museums and art galleries.

NATIONAL MUSEUM OF AFRICAN ART

Part of the Smithsonian Institute, this museum highlights African art and culture from ancient times to the present. The museum displays textiles, ceramics, tools, instruments, masks, furniture, and art techniques such as painting, print making, sculpture, and pottery to show the diversity of art throughout Africa.

NATIONAL MUSEUM OF AMERICAN HISTORY

Part of the Smithsonian Institute, this museum has over 3 million artifacts that paint a picture of American History. The artifacts fit into 28 different collections including sports and leisure, photography, work, transportation, music, family and social life, and popular entertainment to name a few.

NATIONAL MUSEUM OF NATURAL HISTORY

Part of the Smithsonian Institute, this museum has over 125 million natural science specimens such as insects, fish, and plants and also many cultural artifacts. The museum is the size of 18 football fields.

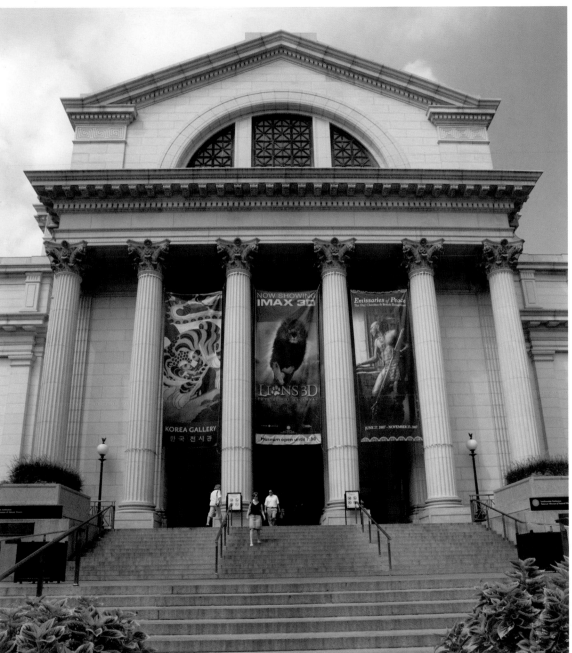

NATIONAL MUSEUM OF THE AMERICAN INDIAN

Part of the Smithsonian Institute, this museum highlights the life, literature, language, history, and arts of the Native American Indians. It displays a variety of Native American items that represent their cultural and religious beliefs and daily life.

NATIONAL MUSEUM OF WOMEN IN THE ARTS

The only museum in the world that is solely dedicated to the contributions of women artists. Wilhelmina Cole Holladay, an art historian and collector, founded the museum in 1987. It preserves the work of women and teaches the public about their achievements.

NATIONAL PORTRAIT GALLERY

Part of the Smithsonian Institute, a wide variety of famous Americans are honored here through paintings, prints, sculptures, drawings, and photographs.

NATIONAL REPUBLICAN PARTY

A political party that existed in the United States between 1829-1833. It was started by Henry Clay and was dissolved when the Whig Party joined previous National Republican Party members with some other political groups.

NATIONAL THEATRE

A theatre that has been operating on Pennsylvania Avenue since 1835. Many famous actors have appeared on the stage and even had jobs as an usher or stage door-man at the National Theatre. For a short time the theatre became a movie house, but very quickly returned to live shows. Some people think that the theatre is haunted by the ghost of an actor named John McCullough who was shot by a fellow actor while on stage.

NAVY AND MARINE MEMORIAL

A memorial nicknamed "Waves and Gulls" stands in Lady Bird Johnson Park on Columbia Island. The memorial honors United States Navy Sailors and US Merchant Marines who lost their lives at sea during World War I.

OCTAGON HOUSE

James Madison and his wife, Dolley, temporarily moved into the Octagon House in 1814 when the White House was burned by British soldiers. Today, it is home to The American Institute of Architects and is open to the public for tours.

OLD EXECUTIVE OFFICE BUILDING

A federal office building located next door to the White House. This building is now called the Dwight D. Eisenhower Executive Office Building. Many of the agencies that make up the President's Executive Office such as the Office of the Vice President, the Office of Management and Budget, and the National Security Council are located there.

OLD POST OFFICE

Washington's first skyscraper, this building was the largest and tallest government building in the city. It was built to house the U.S. Post Office and the D.C. Post Office. It was also the first building to have its own electric power plant with engines operating to run its 3,900 lights. Today, the building is #8 of places to see in Washington, D.C. It is full of restaurants, shops, and a variety of music. The granite clock tower stands 270 feet over the street below and gives a great view of the city.

OLD STONE HOUSE

One of the oldest known structures remaining in the city. The Old Stone House is famous for being just an ordinary house. It was built and lived in by common people and today is a tribute to the ordinary and every day life of middle class colonial America.

PENNSYLVANIA AVENUE

Nicknamed "America's Main Street," Pennsylvania Avenue connects the White House and the Capitol. The street is also well known for hosting parades, celebrations, protests, and marches.

PENTAGON

The headquarters of the United States Department of Defense. The building has five sides, five floors above ground and two below ground, and five hallways on each floor that total more than 17 miles. The Pentagon's offices have about 26,000 employees, which is more than any other office building in the world. On September 11th, 2001, exactly 60 years from the day of its groundbreaking, the Pentagon was struck by American Airlines Flight 77 during terrorist attacks on the United States. A memorial is being made to honor the 184 victims who lost their lives.

POTOMAC RIVER

A 413-mile long river that flows through West Virginia, Maryland, Virginia, and Washington, D.C. before emptying into the Chesapeake Bay.

PRESIDENT

The elected head of the United States government, the chief of state, and the Commander-in-Chief of the United States military. Presidents are elected every four years by the electoral college and have a two term limit so that they cannot serve longer than eight years. The President lives in the White House while in office.

QUEEN ISABELLA

Queen Isabella agreed to finance the expedition of Christopher Columbus to the New World. This statue was donated by Spain and is located just outside the Organization of American States Building.

QUICK FACTS ABOUT WASHINGTON, D.C.

Capital city of the United States of America

Motto: *Justitia Omnibus*

Origin of name: Named after George Washington and Christopher Columbus

District's Bird: Wood Thursh

District's Flower: American Beauty Rose

District's Tree: Scarlet Oak

District's Song: Star Spangled Banner

Population = 588,292 (estimate)

Land Size = 68 square miles

REFLECTING POOL

A large pool located between the Lincoln Memorial and the Washington Memorial. The pool reflects these two monuments and is also a place for reflection. With a width of 167 feet, a length of 2,029 feet, and a depth of 18-30 inches this pool holds 6,750,000 gallons of water.

REPUBLICAN PARTY

One of the two major political parties in the United States. The symbol for the Republican Party is an elephant. It is said that the Republican Party is the more socially conservative and economically liberal of the two political parties.

ROBERT E. LEE MEMORIAL

The Arlington House was the plantation estate of Robert E. Lee and his family for 30 years. At different times in history the home was also an army encampment and a community for emancipated slaves. Today, the home stands as a memorial to Robert E. Lee and the grounds are also the home to Arlington National Cemetery.

ROCK CREEK PARK

More than 2,000 acres of land along the Rock Creek Valley is among the oldest of the country's national parks. The park also includes horse trails, a tennis stadium, a nature center, a planetarium, an outdoor place for concerts, picnic areas, and playgrounds.

RONALD REAGAN BUILDING

A federal building named after the 40th President of the United States, Ronald Reagan. When it was built it was the most expensive federal building ever to be constructed. The building hosts over 1,200 events each year and is home to the Department of Homeland Security, Border and Customs Patrol offices, and the US Agency for International Development.

ROSS, BETSY

The woman who some people believe sewed the very first American flag. The first flag had 13 stars and stripes to represent the original 13 colonies. The flag was flown when the Declaration of Independence was read aloud at Independence Hall on July 8, 1776.

ROTUNDA

A circular room in the center of the Capitol Building that connects the House to the Senate. The rotunda is 96 feet wide and 180 feet high with a beautifully painted dome. Each figure painted on the dome is 15 feet high and can be seen clearly from the floor.

SEABEE MEMORIAL

The Seabees Memorial stands outside the main gate of the Arlington National Cemetery. Seabees are members of the construction battalion of the U.S. Navy and are responsible for the construction of roadways, airstrips, and a wide variety of construction projects in combat areas.

SECOND CONTINENTAL CONGRESS

The body of representatives from the original 13 colonies that adopted the Declaration of Independence and the Articles of Confederation. The Second Continental Congress met from May of 1775 to March of 1781.

SECRET SERVICE

A federal law enforcement agency that protects national leaders and visiting foreign leaders. The Secret Service was started in 1865 to put an end to the counterfeiting of American currency. Its headquarters are in Washington, D.C. After the assassination of Robert F. Kennedy during his run for President it was decided that the secret service would also protect Presidential candidates.

SENATE

One of the two chambers that make up Congress. The Senate is made up of two senators from each of the fifty states that serve six-year terms. The Senate proposes and votes on laws.

SMITHSONIAN CASTLE

The Smithsonian's first building, usually just called "The Castle," houses the administrative offices and the Visitor Information Center.

SMITHSONIAN INSTITUTE MUSEUMS

In 1826 a British scientist named James Smithson wrote his will and left his $500,000 estate (worth over $9 million dollars in today's dollars) to the United States "to found at Washington, under the name Smithsonian Institute, an establish for the increase and diffusion of knowledge among men." Today, the Smithsonian Institute has 19 museums and 9 research centers. Some of the museums include The Air and Space Museum, The National Museum of American History, the National Museum of Natural History, the National Zoological Park, The National Museum of African Art, and the National Museum of the American Indian.

SPIRIT OF ST. LOUIS

A plane flown by Charles Lindbergh that made the first non-stop solo transatlantic flight. Lindberg took off from Roosevelt Field in Long Island on May 20th, 1927 and landed in Paris, France 33 hours, 30 minutes, and 29.8 seconds later. *The Spirit of St. Louis* is now on display at the Smithsonian's National Air and Space Museum.

STAR SPANGLED BANNER

A poem written by Francis Scott Key after being held captive during the bombing of Fort McHenry, in Baltimore, Maryland. In the morning Key looked out and saw the American Flag flying high, signaling an American victory, and was inspired to write a poem named "Defense of Fort McHenry." Later the poem was put to music and named *The Star Spangled Banner.* It became the National Anthem on March 3rd, 1931 thanks to a law passed by President Herbert Hoover. The flag that was raised at Fort McHenry is now on display at the Smithsonian's National Museum of American History.

STATUARY HALL

A collection of 100 statues in the Capitol building. Each state has donated two statues of people who have been important in the state's history. The statues were originally displayed in the old hall of the House of Representatives, which was renamed Statuary Hall. The collection outgrew the hall and is now spread throughout the Capitol building.

THEODORE ROOSEVELT ISLAND

Located in the Potomac River just west of the city. The 88 plus acre wooded island is maintained as a natural park, and includes a national memorial to Theodore Roosevelt, the 26th President.

THIRTEEN COLONIES

The British colonies in America that were founded between 1607-1732. These colonies rebelled against British rule and on July 4, 1776 the Declaration of Independence was signed, freeing themselves from Britain. Those 13 colonies were: Province of New Hampshire, Province of Massachusetts Bay, Colony of Rhode Island, Connecticut Colony, Province of New York, Province of New Jersey, Province of Pennsylvania, Delaware Colony, Province of Maryland, Colony and Dominion of Virginia, Province of North Carolina, Province of South Carolina, and Province of Georgia.

THOMAS JEFFERSON MEMORIAL

A memorial built to honor the 3rd President of the United States. The Thomas Jefferson Memorial is in West Potomac Park in the tidal basin of the Potomac River. The memorial is circular with white marble steps, large white columns, and a white domed roof. Inside stands a 19-foot tall, 10,000 pound bronze statue of President Jefferson. Some of Jefferson's famous quotes are written inside the monument.

TIDAL BASIN

A 10-foot deep and over 100-acre inlet that is connected to the Potomac River and the Washington Channel. The inlet helps to flush out the Washington Channel by collecting 250 million gallons of water during high tide in the Potomac and then releasing it into the Channel to move away silt and debris. The water flows through inlet and outlet gates. The Tidal Basin is surrounded by a walkway that winds under beautiful cherry trees that bloom in March or April.

ULYSSES S. GRANT MEMORIAL

A memorial built to honor Civil War General and United States President, Ulysses S. Grant. The memorial consists of a statue of Grant sitting on his horse, Cincinnati. It is the largest equestrian statue in the United States and the 2nd largest in the world.

UNION STATION

The large train station in Washington, D.C. that is considered to be the entrance to the city. When it was first built, it was the largest train station in the world. It was such an important part of the city that a Presidential Suite was used for entertaining and to welcome foreign dignitaries. Union Station is now served by the commuter rail, Amtrak, and Washington Metro buses and trains. Inside the station there is also a movie theater and over 100 places to eat, drink, and shop. Union Station has over 32 million visitors each year and its grand halls are still used for important functions and celebrations.

UNITED STATES BOTANIC GARDENS

A living plant museum established in 1820 and is located today on the National Mall, across from the Capitol.

UNITED STATES CAPITAL

Washington, D.C. became the capital of the United States on July 16, 1790. The location was chosen by George Washington and approved by Congress. Philadelphia, Pennsylvania was the capital city prior to 1790.

UNITED STATES HOLOCAUST MEMORIAL MUSEUM

A museum that serves as a living memorial to the Holocaust, its victims and survivors. The museum has over 900 artifacts for visitors to explore and four theaters that show historic footage and testimonies from eyewitnesses. The museum also provides community outreach and educational services to make sure that this part of history is never repeated.

UNITED STATES PASSPORT

The Bureau of Consular Affairs, located in the Harry S. Truman Building, is responsible for issuing United States passports. A passport proves the identity and nationality of the bearer and is required to enter and leave most foreign countries. The earliest passports were issued to American citizens traveling abroad in 1789.

UNITED STATES NAVY MEMORIAL AND HERITAGE CENTER

A memorial in Market Square that honors those who have served in the Navy, Coast Guard, Marine Corps, and Merchant Marines. The memorial is home to the Lone Sailor statue, the Granite Sea, two fountain pools, a visitor's center, and the Heritage Center with its Arleigh Burke Theater, rotating exhibits about sea services, and the Navy Log.

US SUPREME COURT

The highest court in the Judicial Branch of the Federal Government. It is made up of a Chief Justice and eight other associated justices who all serve for life unless they resign or are impeached. The Supreme Court has the final say in all rulings that they make. If a case is tried in the Supreme Court it cannot be appealed anywhere else.

USS SEQUOIA PRESIDENTIAL YACHT

A floating retreat, the U.S.S. *Sequoia* was used by seven Presidents for shaping some of the most significant decisions of the 20th century. It is a 1925 Trumpy-designed yacht with a large collection of presidential photographs and original memorabilia. The yacht is owned by the Sequoia Presidential Yacht Group, LLC.

VETO

When the President refuses to sign a bill or legislation that has been approved by Congress. Congress can override the President's veto by a two-thirds vote in the House of Representatives and the Senate.

VICE PRESIDENT

A member of the Executive Branch of the Federal Government who ranks immediately below the President. Presidential candidates select a Vice President to run with on a presidential ticket and the two are elected together. If, for any reason, the President cannot continue serving, the Vice President takes over. The Vice President has some official responsibilities including serving as the deciding vote when the Senate is caught in a tie and certifying the vote count of the Electoral College. The Vice President serves as an advisor to the President and usually as the spokesperson for the administration's policies, Chairmen of the Board of NASA, and a member of the board of the Smithsonian Institute. The Vice President lives in a designated home on the grounds of the United States Naval Observatory.

VIETNAM WAR VETERANS MEMORIAL

A memorial that honors the men and women who served the United States during the Vietnam War. The memorial's Wall of Names shows more than 58,200 names etched into black granite panels that represent all of the people who lost their lives or are still missing. Each name is marked with either a diamond, meaning the person died during the war, or a plus sign, meaning they are still missing. The memorial is also home to *The Three Servicemen* statue, three soldiers walking and supporting each other, and the In Memory Plaque, honors soldiers who lost their lives after the war due to injuries which occurred during the war.

VIETNAM WOMEN'S MEMORIAL

A part of the Vietnam War Veterans Memorial, this sculpture shows three uniformed women attending to a wounded soldier. This part of the memorial was dedicated in 1993 to honor all of the women who served in Vietnam.

VIRGINIA FLAG

The state flag of Virginia consists of the state seal centered on a background of blue. The seal depicts a woman, symbolizing courage and virtue, standing over a prostate man, symbolizing tyranny. The commonwealth of Virginia was settled in 1607 and joined the Union in 1788.

VOYAGER

An aircraft that made the first non-stop, non-refueled flight around the world on December 23, 1986. The flight took nine days (and about 3 ½ minutes), covered 24,986 miles, at an average speed of 116 miles per hour, and left from Edwards Air Force Base in California. The *Voyager* is now on display at the Smithsonian's National Air and Space Museum.

WAR OF 1812

A war fought between the United States and Great Britain. The burning of Washington took place when British forces invaded and burned the city in 1814 during the War of 1812. The orders given were to only burn public buildings so family homes were spared, but the White House and other government buildings were destroyed. The burning of Washington was in retaliation for the Battle of York during which U.S. troops burned and looted the Parliament buildings of Upper Canada.

WASHINGTON MONUMENT

This monument is just over 555 feet tall and is shaped like an Egyptian obelisk. It is made of granite, marble, and sandstone and was completed in December of 1884.

WASHINGTON NATIONAL CATHEDRAL

Officially known as the Cathedral Church of Saint Peter and Saint Paul in the City and Diocese of Washington, this building was voted one of the most beautiful in the United States. It has also been designated as the National House of Prayer. It is the sixth tallest cathedral in the world and the second largest in the United States.

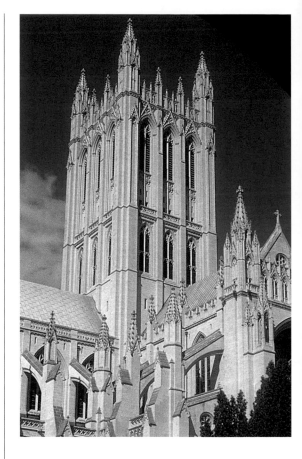

WHIG

British North American Colonists who rebelled against the Crown during the American Revolution. Their revolts led to the establishment of the independent states that became the United States of America. Whig was also a political party that existed between 1833-1856.

WHITE HOUSE

The home and office of the President of the United States. The White House's address is 1600 Pennsylvania Avenue. The first President to live in the White House was the nation's second President, John Adams. The famous oval office was built during the presidency of William Howard Taft in 1909. The West Wing refers to where the offices are located and, in all, the White House has 132 rooms, is 55,000 square feet, and sits on 18 acres of land.

WILLARD HOTEL

A famous Washington hotel that has been home to some historical events and has had many impressive guests. Visitors can see a hotel bill, in the amount of $773.75, paid by President Lincoln with his first paycheck as President. It was also the site of a Peace Conference in 1861 that was an attempt to prevent the beginning of the Civil War. Julia Ward Howe wrote the words to *The Battle Hymn of the Republic* at the Willard and Ulysses S. Grant coined the term "lobbyist" to describe the people who started to make appearances in the hotel's lobby after discovering that Grant like to spend quiet time there. The present day Willard Hotel is a fabulous hotel with a spa, gym, and outdoor café.

WORLD WAR II MEMORIAL

A memorial built to honor the 16 million who served in the U.S. Armed Forces, the 400,000 who lost their lives, and all of those who supported the effort from home. The memorial was opened in April of 2004 and has fifty-six 17-foot tall pillars arranged in a semicircle around a plaza. There are also two 43-foot arches that stand at each end of the semicircle that are inscribed with the words "Atlantic" and "Pacific". The memorial's Freedom Wall has over 4,000 gold stars that each represent 100 lives lost. In front of the wall are the words "Here we mark the price of freedom."

WRIGHT FLYER

The first powered aircraft built by the Wright Brothers. On December 17, 1903 the Wright brothers made four brief flights with the longest one lasting 59 seconds. The Flyer is now on display at the Smithsonian's National Air and Space Museum.

X-15

The rocket-powered North American X-15 set numerous altitude and speed records in the early 1960's and is the fastest aircraft ever flown. It reached the edge of space at an altitude of 67 miles and attained a speed of Mach 6.7. Its last flight was in 1968 and is now on display at the Smithsonian's National Air and Space Museum.

YANKEE

The nickname given to people from the United States who live North of the Mason-Dixon line. New Englanders are most commonly called Yankees. The term is also used for soldiers who fought for the Union during the Civil War.

YANKEE-DOODLE

A well-known American patriotic song. Even though the British used the song as a way to make fun of the American colonists during the Revolutionary War, it became the American colonists' rallying anthem.

YEAGER, CHUCK

A retired General in the United States Air Force. He was also a test pilot and in 1947 he became the first pilot to travel faster than sound in level flight and ascent. The Bell X-1 that he was piloting is on display at the Smithsonian's National Air and Space Museum.

ZIP CODE

A code that identifies a U.S. Post Office mailing area. "Zip" stands for Zone Improvement Code. The White House uses the zip code 20500.

ZOO

The Smithsonian's National Zoological Park, more commonly known as the National Zoo, is a 163-acre home to over 2,000 animals from close to 400 different species. The Zoo is also a research, conservation, and education center dedicated to endangered animals and has a state-of-the-art veterinary hospital.

Smithsonian *National Zoological* Park

Been There, Done That!

STICKER SHEET

Now that you have seen the historic monuments, learned all the interesting facts, and visited the fun attractions of Washington, D.C., it's time to mark where you've been and what you've done. Simply, match the places on the stickers to their correct location on the map to create your own personal guide around our capital.

**The
White House**

**Washington
Monument**

**Jefferson
Memorial**

**Lincoln
Memorial**

U.S. Capital

The Pentagon

**National Air
& Space Museum**

**Smithsonian
Institute**

**National
Aquarium**

**Vietnam Veterans
Memorial**

**Arlington
National Cemetery**

**Museum of
American History**

**Museum of
Natural History**

**U.S. Navy
Memorial**

**National Gallery
of Art**

**Dr. Martin Luther
King, Jr. Library**